Max Woody
Chair Maker

A Legacy in Wood

For Stephanie Bagwell

Best Wishes

Max Woody   July 25 2015

Happy Birthday!

To Stephanie

Honor your own heritage.

Julia Taylor Ebel

7-25-15

Other Books by Julia Taylor Ebel

Addie Clawson: Appalachian Mail Carrier

Dresses, Dreams and Beadwood Leaves

Jack Tales and Mountain Yarns, as Told by Orville Hicks

Hansi and the Iceman

Mama's Wreaths

Orville Hicks: Mountain Stories, Mountain Roots

The Picture Man

Walking Ribbon

Max Woody
Chair Maker

A Legacy in Wood

Julia Taylor Ebel

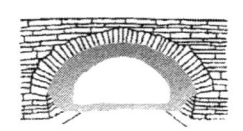

Parkway Publishers, Inc.
Blowing Rock, NC

Copyright 2015 | Julia Taylor Ebel

Photographs are by Julia Taylor Ebel unless otherwise credited. Efforts have been made to identify the photographic sources. Corrections will be made in subsequent printings if additional information about the photographers' identity is made available to the author.
Julia Taylor Ebel, P.O. Box 11, Jamestown, NC 27282

Library of Congress Cataloging-in-Publication Data

Ebel, Julia Taylor.
 Max Woody chair maker : a legacy in wood / Julia Taylor Ebel.
     pages cm
 Summary: "Max Woody is a woodworking craftsman from Marion, North Carolina. This book is his biography and a discussion of his legacy"-- Provided by publisher.
 Audience: 10.
 Audience: Grade 4 to 6.
 ISBN 978-1-5117-5024-0 -- ISBN 1-5117-5024-3
 1. Woody, Max--Juvenile literature. 2. Chair-makers--North Carolina--Marion--Biography--Juvenile literature. 3. Furniture making--North Carolina. I. Title.
 TT197.5.C45E24 2015
 684.10092--dc23
 [B]
                        2015020710

ISBN-13: 978-1511750240 | ISBN-10: 1511750243

Front cover photograph © Jon Perry
Back cover photographs © Jon Perry and Julia Taylor Ebel
Book design by Aaron Burleson, spokesmedia

PRINTED IN THE USA

Especially for Max and Pat,
Myron and Carey

And for all who preserve the treasures of the past
through knowledge, skills and stories

And in memory of Daddy,
who let me tinker with his tools—his plane, his saw, his brace and bit

—JTE

In the shadows of North Carolina's Blue Ridge Mountains, Max Woody has made traditional chairs since 1950. He carries on a long tradition of woodworkers and chair makers before him.

Acknowledgments

What an honor to work with Max Woody and to share his story of the legacy and circumstances that shaped his life. His lifelong commitment to an uncommon purpose speaks a timeless message of encouragement to us all. My thanks to Pat, his wife, who talked with me at Turtle Island and led me to Max, and who patiently gathered photographs.

Thanks to Alan, my husband, who knew I had to write this book, drove to Marion with me, and listened patiently from a rocking chair as Max talked and I scribbled notes.

Thanks to Sandra Greene, who read the manuscript with interest and a critical eye…to Aaron Burleson, who takes my words and images, then meshes them beautifully. Thanks also to Rao Aluri of Parkway Publishing, who first saw that I had stories to keep and who still offers his support.

—Julia

Thanks to my wife and family for being there…and to the many friends who have helped me along the way—too many to name. Working on this book with Julia has been a blessing from God for her kindness and understanding of this old man. Thanks to Alan for his patience as this work was done.

—Max

Wood...

from trees in the Blue Ridge Mountain forests

to chairs made in Max Woody's workshop

to homes near and far

Eyes focused, unwavering…hands steady as steel

Max Woody, Chair Man

"These chairs I make
will last a hundred years, at least,"
the chair man says.

How does he know?

"I know because
the chairs my granddad made
are that old."
He points out some.

"I make my chairs
the way my granddad did."
Square pegs in a round hole,
that's what Max does.
No nails.
No glue.

"I mix my own finish."
He lists ingredients.
"Of course, you can buy it,"
he allows
and names a few brands,
"but I make mine."

Max shows his box of photographs,
chair after chair,
no two exactly the same.

"I make them to fit," he says.

"If you put your arm down
like this,
the arm on your chair
should be right where your arm hits.

"I make a wider seat
for someone more ample."

He takes pride in his work—
and he takes his time.

I never had a hobby, but if I did,
I'm sure it would be making chairs.

Max Woody's signature six-slat rocker,
made from spalted maple

The toolbox made by Max's dad

His Dad's Toolbox

By the time Max came along,
the toolbox was no longer new.

His dad made it in 1916,
a poplar trunk
filled with sundry tools
to meet a man's needs
and tickle a boy's curiosity.

Max explored
the intriguing box,
a treasure chest filled
with hammers and mallets,
level, plane, and square,
chisels and saws.

He tinkered with tools,
hammered on wood
until his dad put a lock on the box,

so Max simply learned
to slip the pin from the hinges
to reach the tempting tools.

Building a Barn

Max was still a boy
when he built a barn with his granddad
and strong bonds with his crippled dad.

He was still a boy,
just 12 years old,
but strong enough
to lift and haul heavy lumber
200 feet or more
as his dad could only watch.

Max and his granddad
planned and measured,
sawed and hammered,
built a feed room and two stalls,
leaving one as a workshop
where Max's dad
would build chairs.

An Ox Named Duck

That same year,
Max raised a black and white calf,
then trained the grown ox
to plow a field.

"Duck was like a pet;
he'd follow me around
about like a dog."
Max recalls those days
and smiles.

A gritty team,
Max and Duck would work the field,
then head back home along the road.

"I'd throw myself across him
like a sack of oats
and ride him—

I'd ride him backwards.
He was my buddy."

Solace Among Tools

Max was 15
when his dad died
and the undertaker brought
the lifeless body home
to wait for burial.

Needing space to himself
and nearness to his dad,
Max found solace
in the presence of memory—
in the barn
he'd helped to build.

In the workshop there,
Max oiled his dad's tools.
With a blackboard eraser
dipped in oil,
he moved his hands
slowly, carefully
over tools and memories
of the father he deeply loved.

A collection of old tools at Max's workshop

Changes

With three sisters
and a widowed mother,
Max shouldered duties
as the man of the house.
Tending milk cows,
chickens and pigs,
he stayed in school.

At 15,
Max caught a train to Johnson City
for summer work
at a hardwood flooring plant.

At 16,
he broke a horse to plow,
farmed as a sharecropper,
worked a summer job,
digging ditches
on the road to Mt. Mitchell
with shovel, pick,
and pure strength.
When corn was ripe,
he managed the harvest.

With graduation coming,
one teacher saw his future
with shallow hope.
Another saw promise
and the heavy weight he bore.
With kindness and guidance
she helped him graduate.

Seasoned by work
and earthy skills,
Max looked ahead.
He'd carve his own path.

Max's dad made this digging tool from a car spring.

Max's Dreams

Through factory jobs
and road work,
Max traded hard labor
for dollars and dreams.

He saved his earnings
and looked ahead
toward making chairs
as his dad had done,
as his granddad still did,
as other Woody men had done
through five generations or more.

Max could have bought a car,
but when the time was right,
he took his money
on a bus to Charlotte,
bought his first lathe
and other tools,
and had them shipped home.

Max Woody was twenty-one years old
and owner of a fine lathe
that would turn chair posts
with the cycle of days and years
as reliably
as the turning
of earth and moon
and seasons.

Max turns a chair post on his first lathe, February 2015.
His first tools still serve him well.

The First Lathe

For three years after graduation, Max used the Postal Savings Plan to save earnings from work at Drexel Furniture Company. The manufacturing process was not the process he would learn from his grandfather—not the process he would choose to use for making chairs. In 1950, he bought his first lathe, table saw, drill press, band saw, and jointer. With $735 invested in tools and a little money kept to buy wood, he set out to learn the skills he would need for his own chair-making business.

Bowing Chair Backs on a Frame

Chair backs are sawed and then bowed for strength. Slats sawed from the outer part of the log (where the grain is widest) are soaked in boiling water for about an hour. While hot and wet, the wood is flexible and fibers can be slipped a little. From the water, the slats are placed immediately into a bending brake to press the bow into the wood. The bent slats are then laced through a frame with three poles. Adjacent slats are woven on opposite sides of the poles. The slats on the frame are air dried for about two weeks, after which the wood holds the bent shape.

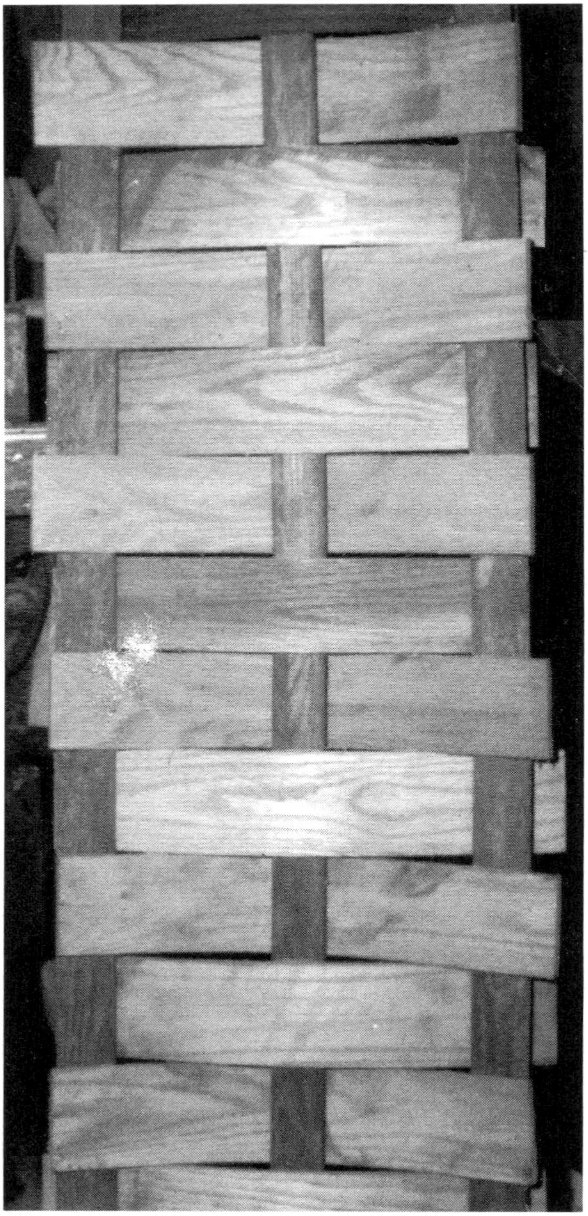

Learning

Max set his mind on making chairs.
He told his granddad
he wanted to work—
to learn the skills.
So he watched his elder's skillful hands
shaping spindles on the lathe.
Together, soon,
they'd cut chair backs.

Yet alone in the workshop
on his first day of work,
Max learned his own way
and figured out how to saw chair backs.
When his granddad returned,
Max showed him
freshly cut slats.

Wood piece
by wood piece,
Max unveiled
the depth of his dreams.

Digging in Marion

"I was always working on something,"
Max says.

When his family bought a house
set on rocks and poles
and built on a slope,
Max saw the prospects
and dug a hole under the house.
He was 14, when he built a cellar
to store the food they'd canned,
tucked in with quilts
and snug beneath the winter chill,

Then Max kept digging.

With dirt dug from under the house,
he built a driveway
before they had a car.
After a couple of years,
he put down his shovel and pick
with enough space cleared
to add three rooms beneath the house.
With his granddad's help,
he built those rooms.

When they needed a ditch
to drain from the house,
Max dug again.
Through a farm program,
he learned to manage
ditching dynamite,

so he used it safely
and quickly made his ditch.

My family would write to me while I was in Korea and tell me that they thought of me when they went to the mailbox because the tree roots were still on the power wires.

Max in Korea, 1951-52. *Courtesy of the Max Woody Collection, photographer unknown*

War and Wood

War surged in Korea,
and Max was called to serve.

The Army found him handy,
watched him use a saw
and build a desk
at Fort Leonard Wood,
then sent him off, a combat engineer
building bridges and roads,
laying mine fields
ahead of troops.

Wood and tools were friends to Max.
Through rice patties,
he built corduroy roads,
using logs cut nearby
from mountain trees.
With fir shipped from Oregon,
he built culverts
so troops could pass.
    First the boards,
      next, local poles,
    and then the soil.

When winter came,
with hindering snow,
Max sawed wood,
built a plow,
and scraped the paths
so troops could move.

In his whole company,
only Max could file saw teeth
to sharpen saws—
a skill he learned at home.

In Korea two final weeks,
Max was called from the deadly fray
on Heartbreak Ridge.
His task—
to file saw after saw
so work could go on
after he went home.

I'd look at the saw teeth I was filing so long that my eyes would get blurry and I'd have to walk away a while.

Max returned home safely with the rank of Staff Sergeant. He realizes that he could have been in the throes of fierce conflict and, perhaps, not returned home if he had not been assigned the critical marathon task of methodically sharpening saws so the combat engineers' work could continue.

Max and his snow plow in Korea,
winter of 1951-52. *Courtesy of the Max Woody
Collection, photographer unknown*

At Fort Leonard Wood, the fatherly Captain Bunis remarked to Max that he had never seen anyone else saw using the whole length of saw teeth. Max explained that if those teeth were not intended to be used, they would not have been put there.

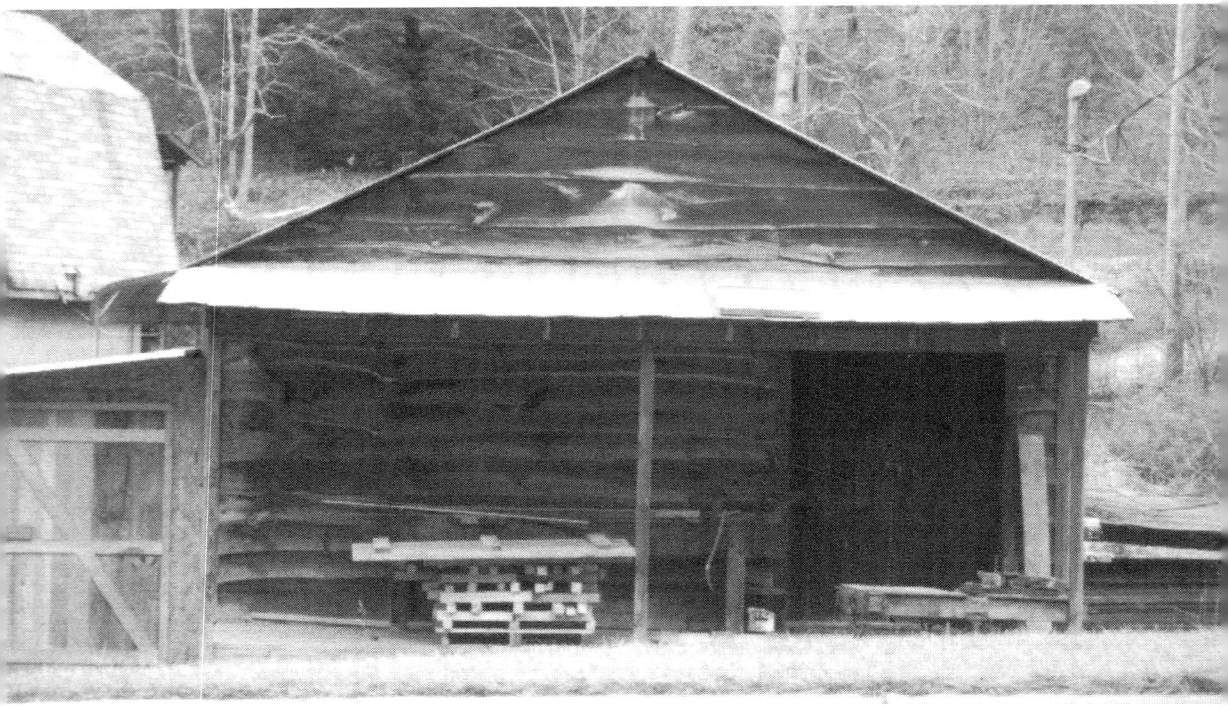

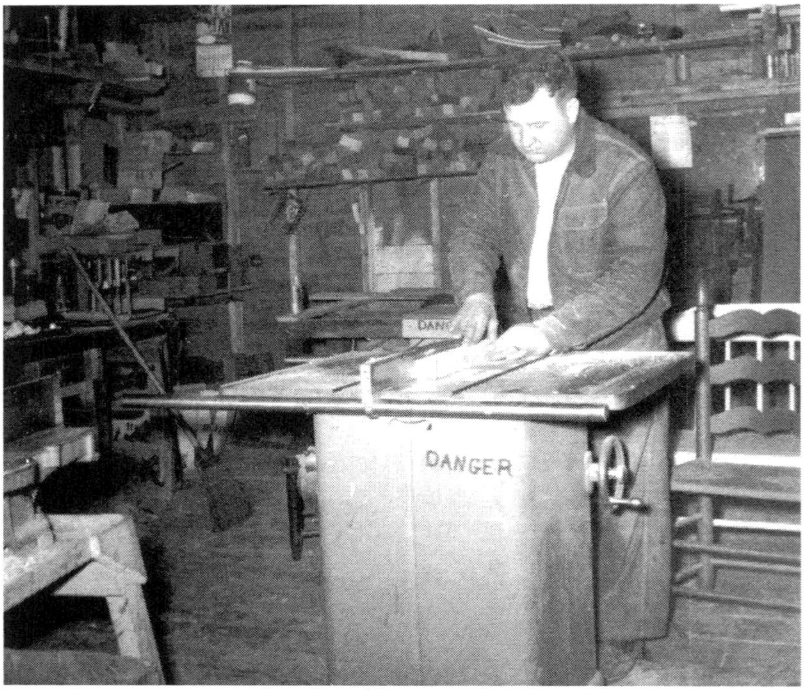
DANGER

Home Again

Service time completed,
Max came home to wood
and worked again—
fully a partner—
beside his skilled granddad.

In just three years,
Max built a shop beside his home
where he could work
and use his own tools
and hang his own shingle.

Max Woody Chair Shop

Ready for business.

In the evenings after a day's work with his granddad, Martin Woody, Max built his first workshop and began making chairs here in 1955. The building now displays his chairs, stools, and benches. The small room to the left is still a workshop. Below, Max in his workshop, 1957.
Photos courtesy of Max Woody, photographer unknown

Desire

"It doesn't take a lot of skill
to make a chair,"
Max says.
"What it takes
is desire."

Max holds a deep well of desire
rooted in a legacy of wood,
enough desire
to build chair
   after chair
      after chair.

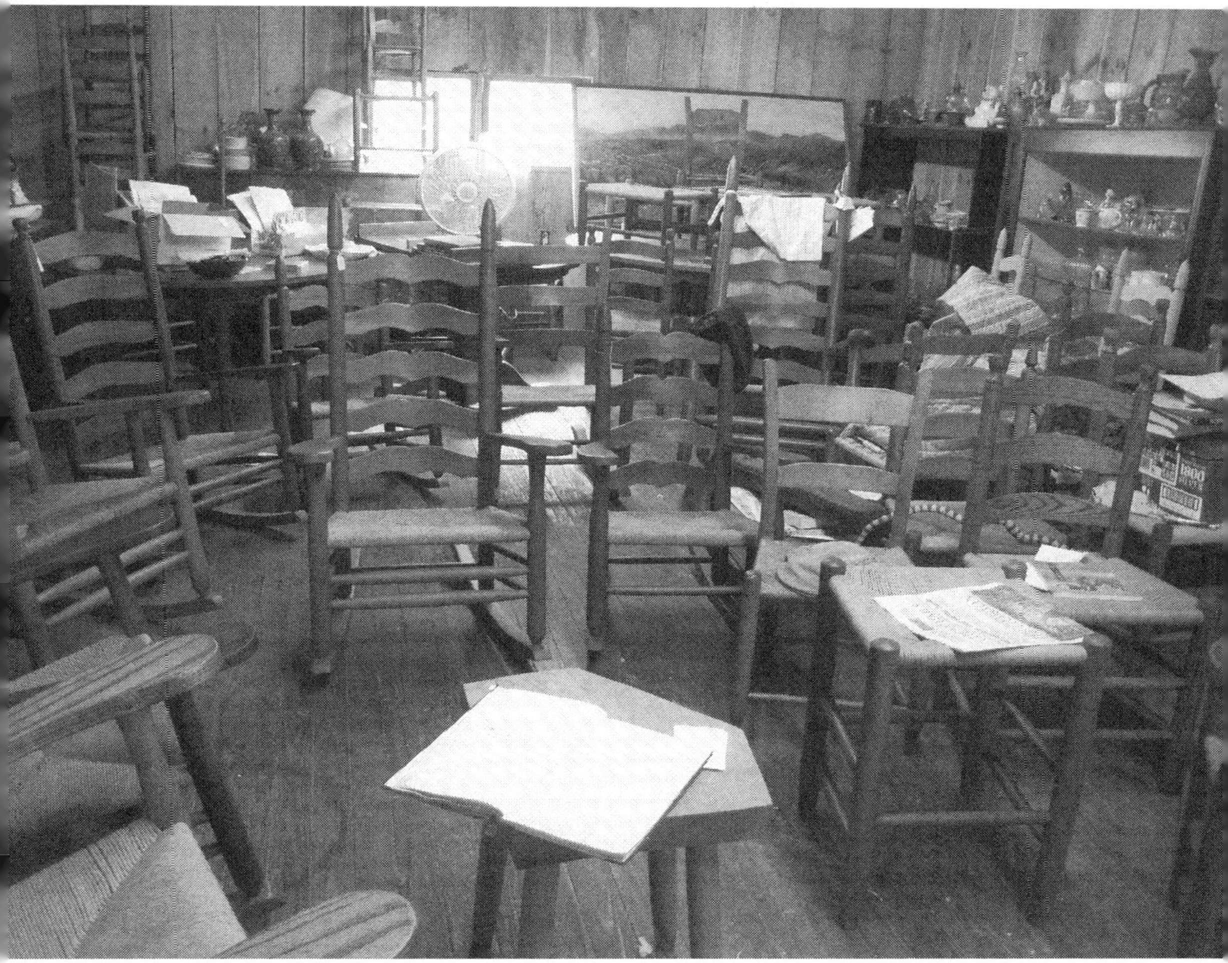

Wood Chips

When his dad drilled holes
with a brace and bit,
Max watched,
intrigued,
as the turning bit
drew corkscrews of wood
from within the hole.

He watched slivers of wood
curl from a plane
gliding over boards.

"When you've got a saw
really sharp,
the sawdust falling out
is beautiful."

Year after year,
as his own lathe turns,
chips fly,
covering Max's hands,
covering his sleeves,
blanketing the floor.

At home with wood chips,
Max watches,
still marvels.

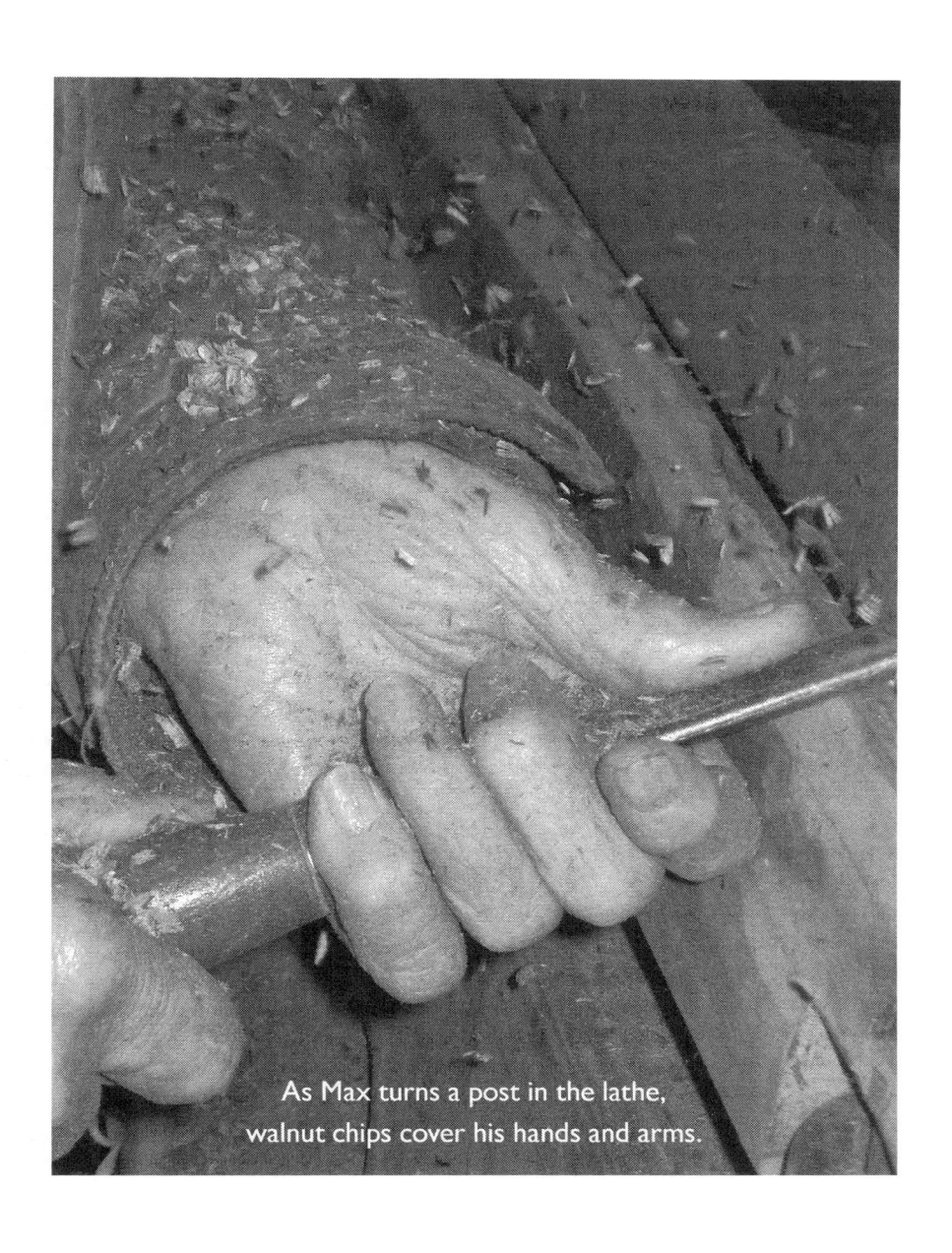

As Max turns a post in the lathe, walnut chips cover his hands and arms.

I never cease to be amazed by chips flying off the lathe—no two alike, like waves rolling in from the sea.

Timeless

A string of years have passed
since Max first turned chair posts
and sawed chair backs.

"In all these years,
I've never had a job," he says.
"I've had a love."

A love of wood.
A love of making chairs.

That's what Max does.
He makes chairs.
He always has.

Making chairs takes time,
plenty of time.

In Max's chairs
you see his love
in form and care,
in craftsmanship.

You feel his love
in the smooth finish of wood.
His chairs are timeless
and strong—
strong enough to outlast us all—

each a monument
to what is genuine and true,
to care,
to heritage,
to time.

No, Max doesn't have a job.
He has a love.

And all of his days are good.

*All my days are good days,
and some are better than others.*

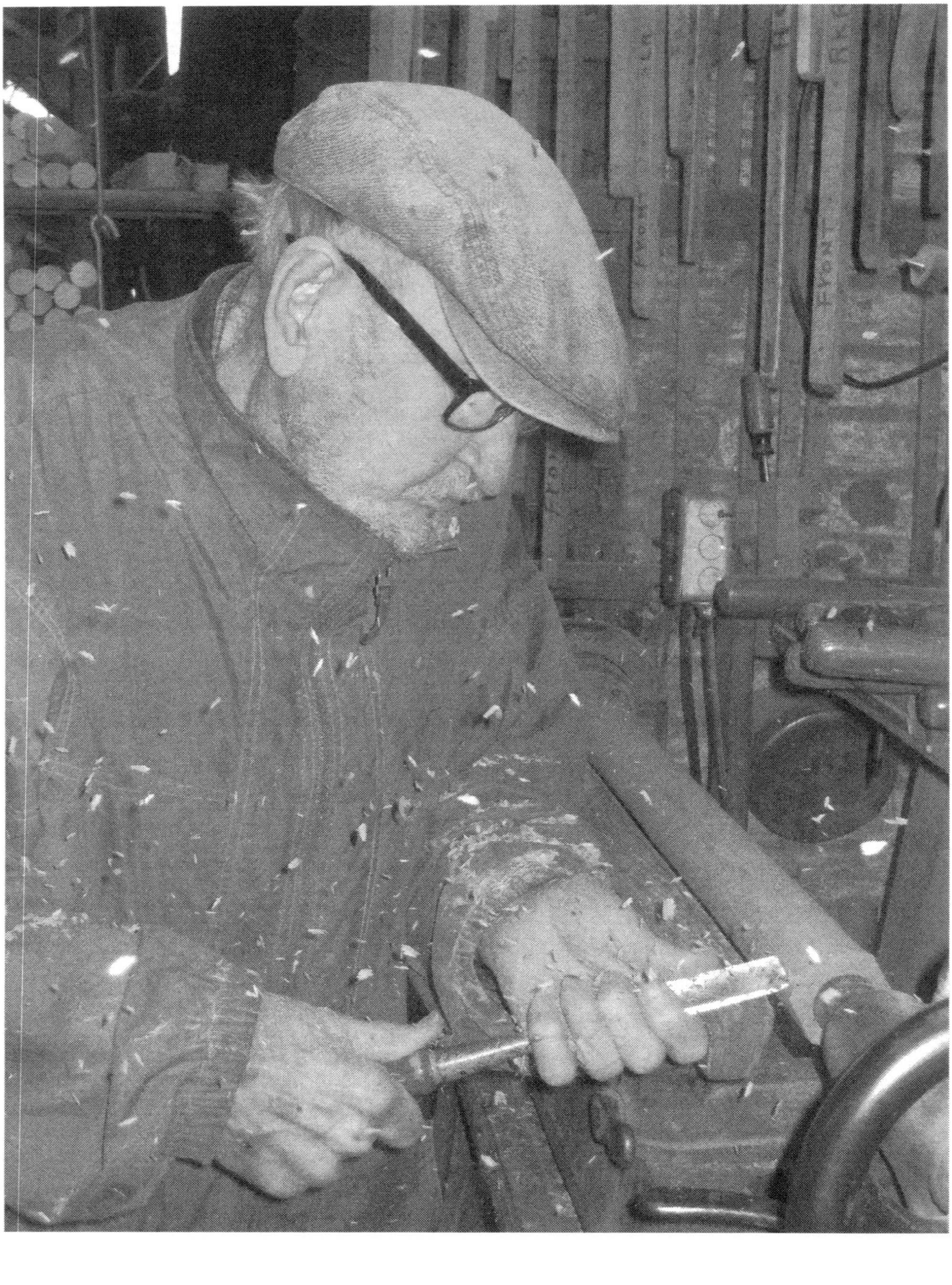

Max's Time

After all these years,
Max has trimmed
his time at the shop,
first to half time,
now a little less.

Half time—
by Max's time—
is twelve hours a day,
six days a week,
off on Sundays.

But no one keeps a clock.
No need to keep a clock
if you love what you do.

A Workshop of Wood

High and low, all around,
Max's shop is a maze of wood—
stacks and racks,
shelves and piles
of wood.

Walnut, maple,
cherry, ash,
rough wood,
turned wood,
boards and poles—

a wealth of wood
ready and waiting
as Max chooses
one piece here
and another there
to build a fitting chair.

Max thinks about the person who'll someday own the chair and plans the chair to match the person.

Bent wood for chair backs

Chair posts in the workshop

Local Wood

No tropical rainforest wood shipped in.
No wood imported.

No wood hauled from Oregon,
Mississippi, or Maine.

Just local Blue Ridge Mountain wood
sawed at local mills.

Same as his granddad used…
and his dad.

Local wood
for traditional chairs.

Of course.

Turning Chair Posts

The lathe spins.
In Max's skilled hands,
gouges and chisels—
handles color keyed
red, white, and blue—
move across turning wood
as square becomes round.
He shapes smooth lines
and gentle curves.

Walnut chips fly,
heap on his hands,
pile on his sleeves
as if they were a part of Max himself.
He leaves them where they land,
no need to brush them off.

Max reaches over turning wood,
wraps fingers around,
and measures by feel
until the size and curves are right.

Again and again, he checks his wood,
slides his hands across the post,
no longer hard,
not splintery and rough,
but soft from turning,
downy and knapped
like a flannel shirt.

No fancy tools used here
to make each post the same.
Max measures each
by hand
and heart.

Cathedrals in wood

Cathedrals

Max picks up a piece of wood,
rough and unfinished.
"You can't see inside wood," he says.
Perhaps that mystery
lures Max to wood.

As chisels and lathe unveil the grain,
he finds beauty in freshly-cut wood,

"See these points in the grain," he says,
noting a chevron along a post.
Cathedrals, he calls them.
"They should point up.
They're prettier that way."

He looks at the post,
takes it out of his lathe,
turns it around,
and sets the post back in the lathe,
reversed,
with cathedrals reaching up
toward the finial waiting to be shaped—
and later,
toward the sky.

Once Max saw cathedrals on a wooden cross in a church,
but they pointed down. "It didn't feel right," he reflects.

Fine Tuning

Max guides turned wood
across a sanding belt
in slow
and measured moves,

then lifts it quickly,
    looks,
decides what's next,
    sands,
looks,
    repeats,
repeats,
    repeats,
until he's satisfied
with every line
and curve.

Smoothing wood with a sanding belt

Court Call

The day the judge lost his gavel
and refused to open court without it,
the clerk of court knew what to do
and called Max Woody,

who set his lathe in motion,
turned handle and mallet for a new gavel,
and had them assembled
in thirty minutes flat,

just in time for the dispatched deputy
to drive to Max's shop
and hurry back to the courthouse
with the new gavel

so the judge
could properly open court

in dignified fashion,
same as usual.

Open Door

The door to Max's shop is open.
Step in
amidst the wood and work
and wood chips
swept in a pile.

Step in
to a place of wonder
that weaves legacy
with now…
right now.

Look,
listen,
and learn.

Beyond Chairs

Max leads the curly-haired girl
and her brother
down the steps to his workshop.

While they watch,
Max sets a post in the lathe,
chooses his tools,
and begins work.

Chips fly
and cover Max's hand,
as a rolling pin takes shape.

A little off here,
a little more there…
sanding here,
sanding there.

And now a bat.
"Let's see how big your hand is,"
Max tells the boy,
who shows his hand.

In an hour or so,
the boy has a bat,
the girl, a rolling pin,

each made to fit,
made just for them
by Max.

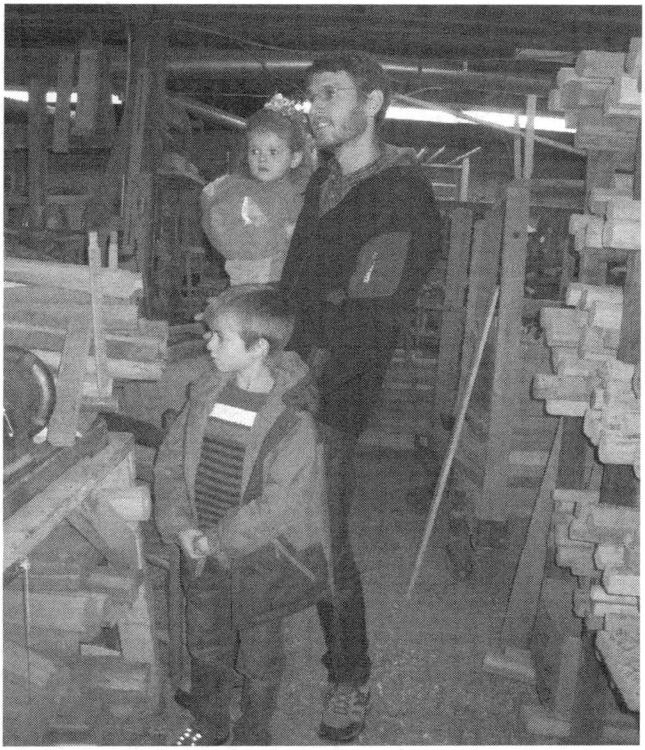

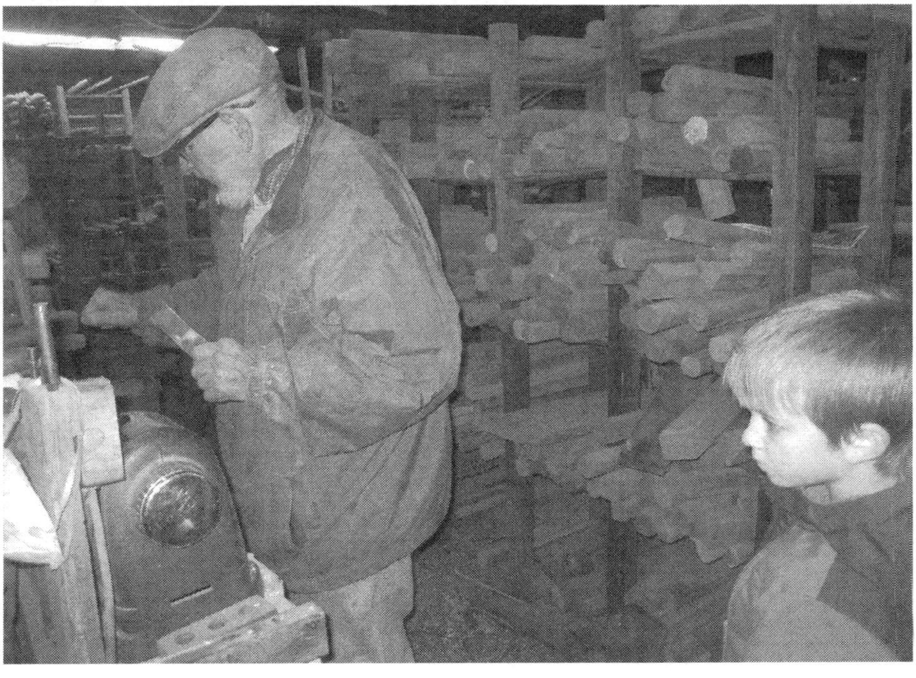

Choosing wood

Familiar with Wood

People who work with wood
need to know wood—
and trees.
Max knows most local trees.
"White pine limbs
grow horizontal from the trunk,"
he explains,
"but the tips lift up."

He knows which trees make sturdy furniture:
maple, walnut,
cherry, ash.
Oak is strong.

White oak makes long-lasting strips
to weave a seat.

Ash is fine for baseball bats.
For ax handles, use hickory or ash.
Locust for fence posts and rails.
Sourwood for sleds.

"There aren't many lin trees any more.
Some people call it *lin;*
it's really *linden,*" Max explains.
"We don't see yellow pine either—
not like we used to."

Lost to borers.

Collector of Wood

Max collects wood.
What else would he collect,
except old tools,
old chairs,
and, yes, friends?

He has samples of wood—
not for chairs—
that came from across the world.
"A pilot friend
brought me wood
from South America."

Max's wood comes from England,
Australia, and France,
from Russia, Holland, and more.

"There's a wood called purple heart.
It's so hard that it has been used
to make bearings for stream ships
when metal was not available."

Max's wood has stories.
If you like to talk about wood,
mention it to Max,
and sit back for a spell
in a Max Woody rocking chair.

Improvisation

Max is a master at making do,
not simply making do,
but using what he has
and making it better.

He gets curious
and figures out
how to make what he needs,
whether of metal or wood.

Perhaps Max learned
from his dad or granddad
or the teacher
who took Max under his wing
and let him tinker in the school workshop…

or perhaps Max just knew
that life doesn't come prepackaged
with all the pieces
and all the tools…

but with enough pieces,
curiosity,
and wit.

If you take time to think, you can do
   nearly anything you wish to do.

Words

Manufacture is a big word
often spoken
about chairs and other things,

but Max's chairs
have no need
for such a soul-less word.

Max operates the mortise machine (the "stomping machine"), which belonged to his grandfather. "It was obsolete when he bought it in 1938," Max says, but the machine has served Max well since he acquired it in 1956.

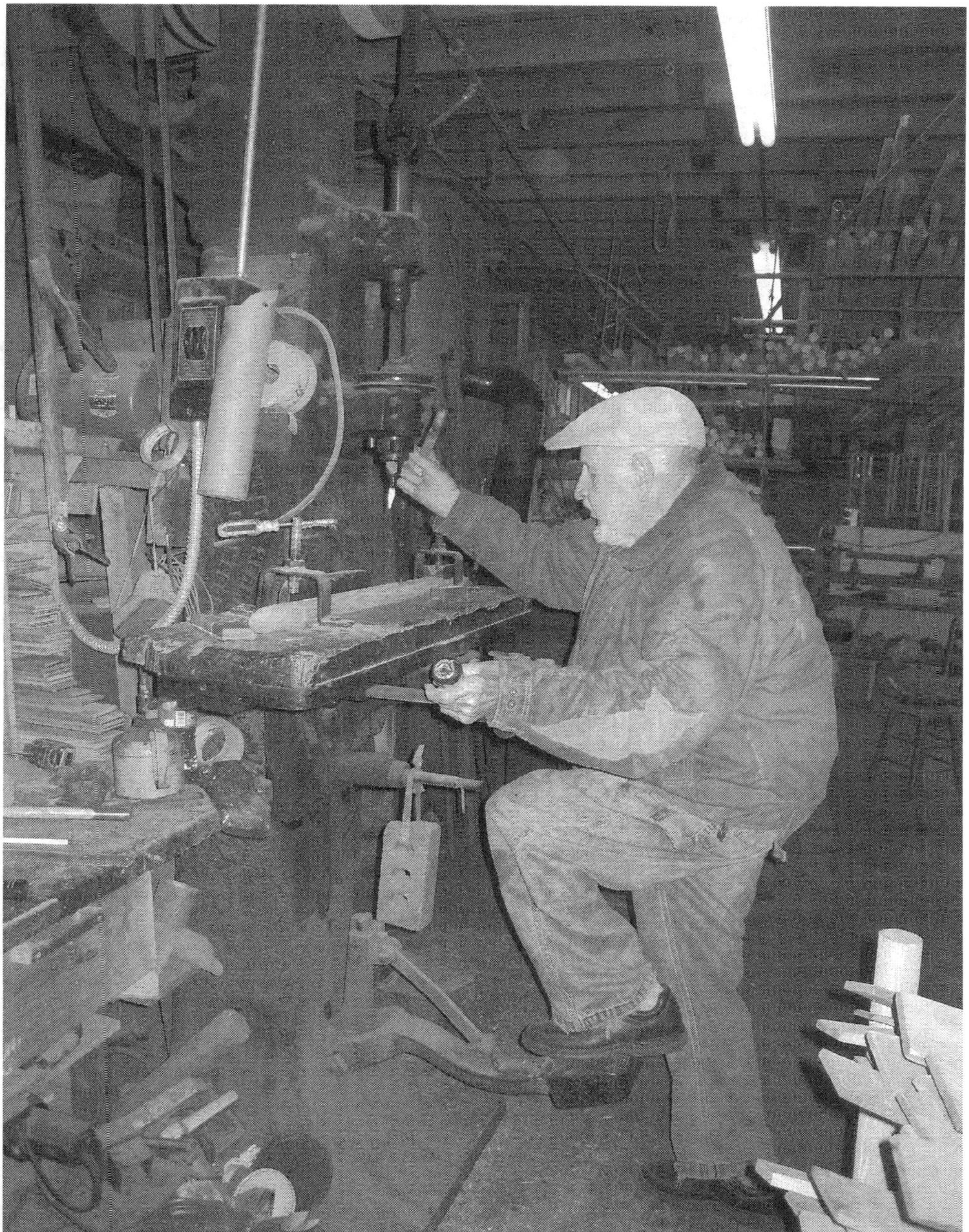

Rounding edges on a rocking chair arm

Satin

Max speaks
in a voice slow and smooth,
smooth
like lines and finish
of fine wood
touched by caring hands,
unhurried hands
that turn rough form
into smooth.

Change takes time
whether in people or wood.
Don't rush.
Don't hurry.
Saw, turn, sand, smooth
until rough wood
becomes satin.

Bringing Up Chair Makers

Myron and Carey
weren't big enough
to stand on a bucket and reach the lathe,
not big enough to turn wood anyway
when they began to come
to their daddy's shop.

After school, on Saturdays,
they were often there
among the wood and chips and tools.
They swept chips and sawdust,
picked up and put up,
and set out chairs for display.

And as they grew,
Max taught them skills
long ago passed on to him.
Soon they sanded,
rubbed oil on wood
and make it shine.

Before his time, Myron
mastered turning on the lathe.
Carey sanded and finished wood
to highlight color and grain.

Another generation of chair makers
grown,
keeps a legacy of wood.

Myron, below, now a skilled chair maker, first learned to use the lathe as he stood on a bucket to reach the turning wood. Carey, shown with Max, focused on finishing wood.
Photos courtesy of the Max Woody Collection, photographer unknown

Helping Hands

"I had so many people
to help me along the way,"
Max recalls and names a few—
his parents,
his granddads…
the teacher Margaret Miller,
who helped him graduate…
the vocational agriculture and shop teacher,
Richard Roberts,
who taught him how
to prune an orchard,
hone and oil tools,
and castrate a pig.

And so, in turn,
Max offers a hand—
again and again.

Max is a giver
who offers many gifts.

Direction

Through decades
and still,
Max opens workshop doors
and welcomes youth.
He shows them his work,
then sits with them,
tells them stories,
    and talks.

He talks about direction,
about their life path.
He warns them that money
is not the goal.

"Do what you love," he tells them.
"If you're not happy in what you're doing,
your life has not been a success."

Simple words of wisdom
from a chair maker who knows,
a chair maker
who loves to make chairs.

Be sure to choose a work you enjoy. If you are happy in what you do you will do a better job and the money will come.
    —Max Woody

Old Fort Mountain Music

Woody's Chair Shop
was a gathering place
on Friday evenings.
First three, then more
gathered with banjoes,
fiddles and bows.

Folks shared music among chairs
made by Max,
made by his granddad—
some chairs older than anyone there.

A heritage of music,
a heritage of chairs—
a likely mix
for folks who know
the riches of the past.

For thirty years, folks who enjoy Blue Grass and old mountain music have played and sung together as their ancestors did before them. The venue has changed a few times, but the gatherings began at Woody's Chair Shop.

Courtesy of the Max Woody collection, photographer unknown

Max's first workshop, now his showroom
and a small workshop

Visitors

The phone rings in Max's workshop.
"Max Woody's Chair Shop—
Old Man Woody here….
Could you hold on a minute?
I've got people here
from the state of Washington."

From across North Carolina,
from across the states,
from beyond,
people find Max,
and many return.
Word travels.

Some see his simple signs,
his rustic workshop,
his showroom,
and stop.
They talk with Max
and see his chairs,
every part made by hand,

each chair
a humble gem.

Genuine

No cover-up in Max's chairs,
just oils that bring out
beauty in wood.

"You can buy stain,"
Max says,
"but I make my finish
and my polish."
Figures.
That's the way Max works,
like Max himself.
There is no pretense in Max,
no pretense in his chairs.
You have to like that sort of man.
One you can trust.
Genuine.

After sixty-four years,
Max still turns chair posts,
saws and molds curved ladder backs,
sands rockers smooth.
Why stop?
He has worked a lifetime
and still his life's work
is not yet finished.
He has purpose.

Max makes chairs,
fine chairs—
real chairs.
Genuine.

Taking time out for conversation in the workshop

Things That Matter

Honesty,
authenticity,

quality of the work of one's hands,
quality of life,

family,
friends,

strangers,
soon to be friends.

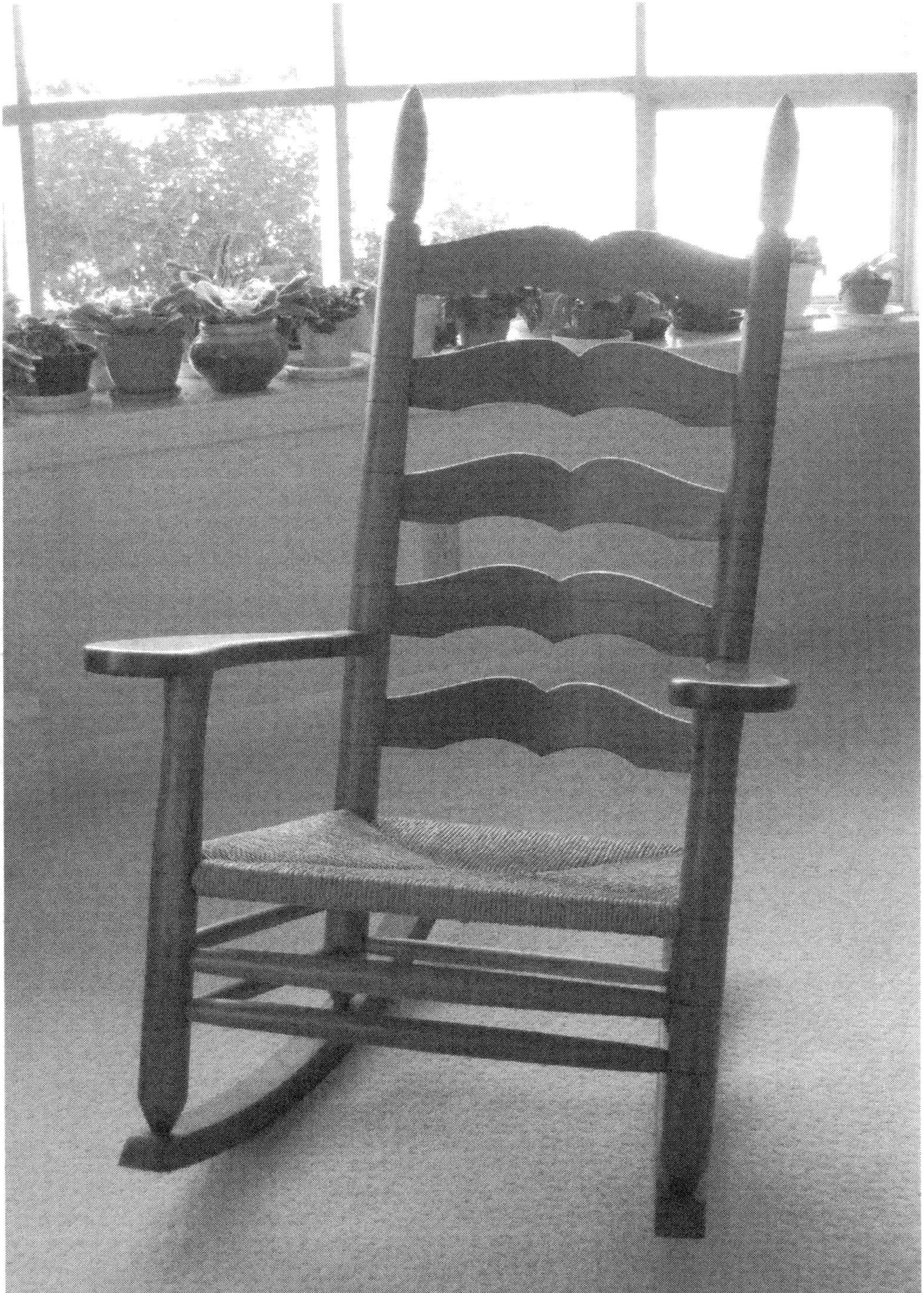

Margaret Woody stands with the pine casket that Max built. His sisters Margaret and Ruth lined it, with help from a close cousin, June Milligan.
Courtesy of the Max Woody Collection, photographer unknown

Resting Place

When his mother died,
Max made a casket,

a fitting place of rest
surrounded by familiar wood

and the scent of a son
steeped in a heritage
of wood.

Max speaks of a gentle and uplifting fellowship among people who gather to build a casket. As they talk, they share memories of the person for whom the casket is made.

Max in the Max Woody Chair Shop, his showroom, on US 221 North, July 2014. Each chair he makes holds stories of its own.

Rocking Chairs

To sit in one of Max's rockers
is to whisper a hush
to a hurried world.

Lean back.
Leave care behind
for a while.
Take time to talk,
   to share,
   to think,
   to read.
Let a lap invite a child.
Tell a story.
Sing a lullaby.

The sturdy rocker holds us up,
steadies us.
Its satin wood and gentle lines
feed our need for beauty,
found honestly here
in wood.

A Hundred Years or So

After sixty-four years,
the lathe still turns.
Chips scatter,
sawdust flies,
and folks stop by
to talk a while…

and Max's chairs
find new homes,
where folks will sit and rock,
talk and read,
where children and grandchildren
will come and go,

and someday take those chairs
to new homes
to rock new generations
for a hundred years
or so.

The Woody Knob Top

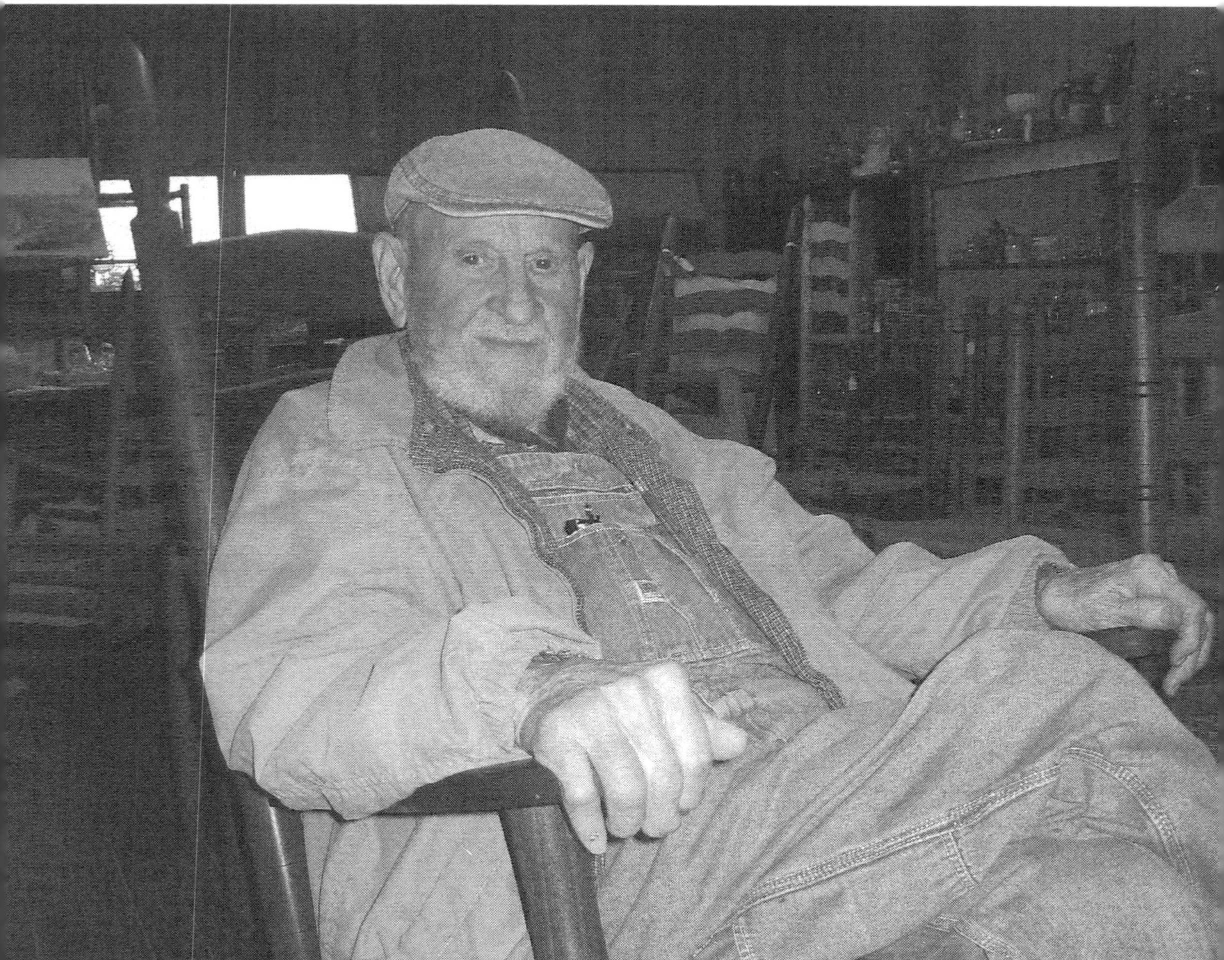

Whispers

With every rock,
   forward, back,
   forward, back,
   forward, back,

Max's smooth voice
still whispers
in rhythm
through satin wood.

   Do what you love.
   Do what you love.
   Do what you love.

Max Woody, Chair Maker

The Shadrack Chair, based on a design by earlier chair maker,
Shadrack Mace, of Madison County

The Dream

Max Woody isn't hard to find. He'll be following his dream—making chairs in the time-honored method of his ancestors. He's likely at his first workshop on US 221 North, near Marion, North Carolina. The shop now includes his showroom and a small workshop. On a sunny day, Max may be working on the porch. If he isn't there, just read the handwritten sign on the door, and call the number mentioned. He might be at his main workshop where the lathes, saws, and other tools are. The unpretentious shop, once a hardware store, is on US 70 West between Marion and Old Fort, North Carolina. The workshop is downstairs below the room where he has sold chairs since 1960.

Max Woody came to woodworking naturally. A sixth generation chair maker, he saw his father making chairs but learned how to make chairs primarily from his grandfather after his father's early death. Left with heavy responsibilities in the family, Max worked whenever he could. He saved money to buy tools, and set out to learn what he needed to know to carry on his woodworking heritage. The creative energies of Max's youth had already taught him to recognize his own potential and to see what results could come from focused effort.

If Max had wanted a prestigious career, he would have pursued other work. If he had wanted a lucrative chair-making business, he would have hired workers, duplicated chair parts, and produced quickly; and he would have hired a marketer. Prestige, production, and big sales were not Max's dreams. His dream was to make traditional chairs by traditional methods and to make them in a way that would reflect not only the hands of the maker but also the persons who would use the chairs. Max has kept that commitment to making chairs one by one, each piece by hand, no duplication.

On the day in June of 1950 when he bought his first woodworking machines, Max took a leap—not a step—onto the path that he would faithfully follow for a lifetime. Max Woody had a dream.

Following the Dream

Max Woody makes traditional ladder back chairs, both rockers and straight chairs. Some are made with the traditional pointed finial, but he also makes a smoother finial, known as the Woody Knob Top. He makes footstools as well. Both necessity and interest have led to other projects. On occasion, he makes a rolling pin for a little girl or for newlyweds; sometimes a bat for a little boy. When a need has occurred, he has made a casket. Once he even made a wooden leg for a man.

Max assembles the handmade pieces of his chairs by age-old methods. He shrink-fits the parts together by placing dried rungs into posts which still hold some moisture. Then he anchors the pieces with a square peg in a round hole. The resulting bond is as strong as the wood itself. The only glue he uses is placed on the joint between the chair arm and the post of a rocking chair.

Max is quick to say that the chairs he builds are necessities of life, not arts and crafts. They are not made to go into museums and galleries. As his ancestors did, he makes real chairs for real people who need chairs. In the past, Max points out, people either made what they needed or bartered with someone who could provide it. The exchange was personal, face to face. Within a community, this cooperation was between neighbors and friends.

For Max, making a chair leads to making friends. When someone visits his shop, the focus is on conversation, not on sales. Then when Max makes a chair for someone, he makes a friend for life. He offers not just a fine-looking and comfortable chair, but also Max himself, a friend. "A lot of people stop back by to see me when they are in the area," Max says. He cherishes these lasting connections and the unexpected visits.

While wood has provided a livelihood for Max, making chairs is not about money. Making chairs reflects his heritage and also who he is and what he values. He finds pleasure in the process and the results of his woodworking. Max cares about wood, about his chairs, and about the people who will use them. These qualities set Max Woody apart as one who works with authenticity and respect for the past and also with compassion and outright love.

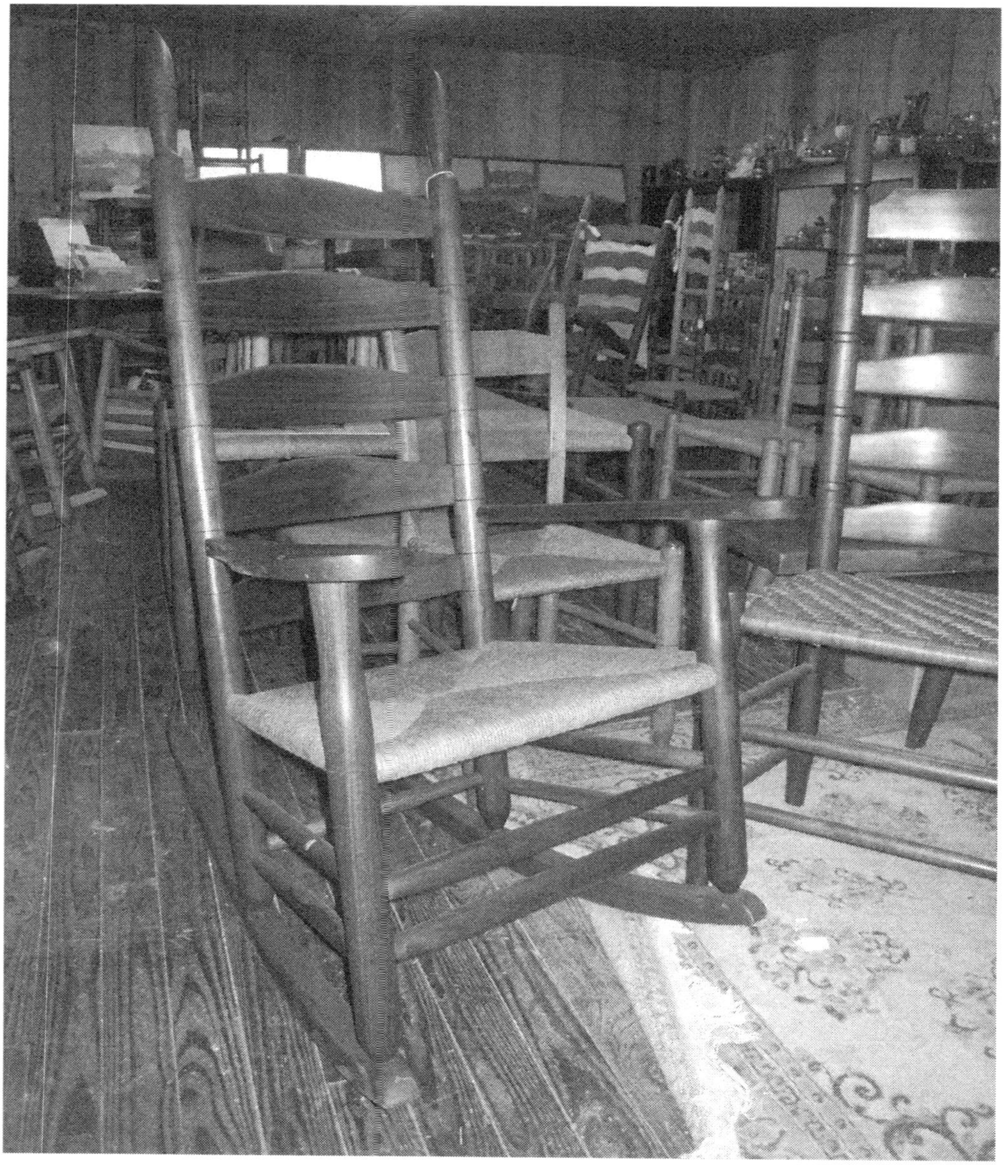

Before Max begins making a chair, he thinks about the person to whom the chair will belong: the personality, the character, the size. Then he makes the chair to fit. The preference of wood, the height of the posts, the slant of a rocking chair, and the length of the arms all determine the chair's character and function. Max's chairs have gone to every state in the nation and to foreign countries as well. The list includes countries as far away as Switzerland, Kuwait, and Japan.

Pieces of Life

Wood and tools have been ever present in Max's life. The wood and tools he used to help his granddad build a barn, the tools he used to dig a massive amount of dirt from under his family's home and then to build three rooms in the opened space, the wood and tools he used in the school shop, the tools he used in boyhood farming—all prepared Max for the days ahead.

Later, wood and tools played a key role in Max's Army experiences. Training in the Missouri Ozarks at Fort Leonard Wood in 1951, he used his practical knowledge, skill with tools, and familiarity with wood. Instead of spending off-duty hours away from the base, he turned to the workshop. He impressed an audience of officers when he reused ammunition boxes to make a desk for the supply room and a cabinet for the mail room. He still has a bench that he made while in service and was able to bring home with him.

In Korea with the 25th Infantry Division as a combat engineer, he built temporary roads, bridges, and culverts for military passage. Earlier, during the summer before his final year of high school, Max also had worked on the construction of the road to Mount Mitchell. In an interesting parallel, his grandfather, Martin Woody, had built wood foundations for culverts along the CC&O Railroad. During the Korean War, Max also used wood in building roads and culverts for the Army's use.

Like the parts of the chairs Max builds, the pieces of his life have fit together and held fast.

A Workshop of Wood, Tools, and Stories

Max's workshop is a place of wonder, filled with the wood that shaped his life. The presence of wood in every corner, high and low, attests to Max's long commitment to making chairs. Inside the workshop, under shelter beside it, and in a building behind it, Max has a collection of local wood that will serve another generation of chair makers.

This wood and his tools are keepers of his story and the stories of the Woody generations before him. His father's handmade toolbox, which fascinated and tempted the young boy Max, remains in Max's workshop. He still uses the first tools that he bought in 1950, and the mortise machine, which Max says was obsolete when his grandfather bought it in 1935, still serves Max well. The machine was made around 1900, but Max acquired it in 1960 as his grandfather retired. The row of hand tools, brace and bit, the color-coded chisels that he painted during Desert Storm—all are parts of the stories.

Max color-coded his chisel handles so he could easily find the ones he needed while the lathe turned. Colors mark the order of use:

Red: gouge • White: round pointed chisel
Blue: skew • Green: parting tool
Yellow: tenoning chisel

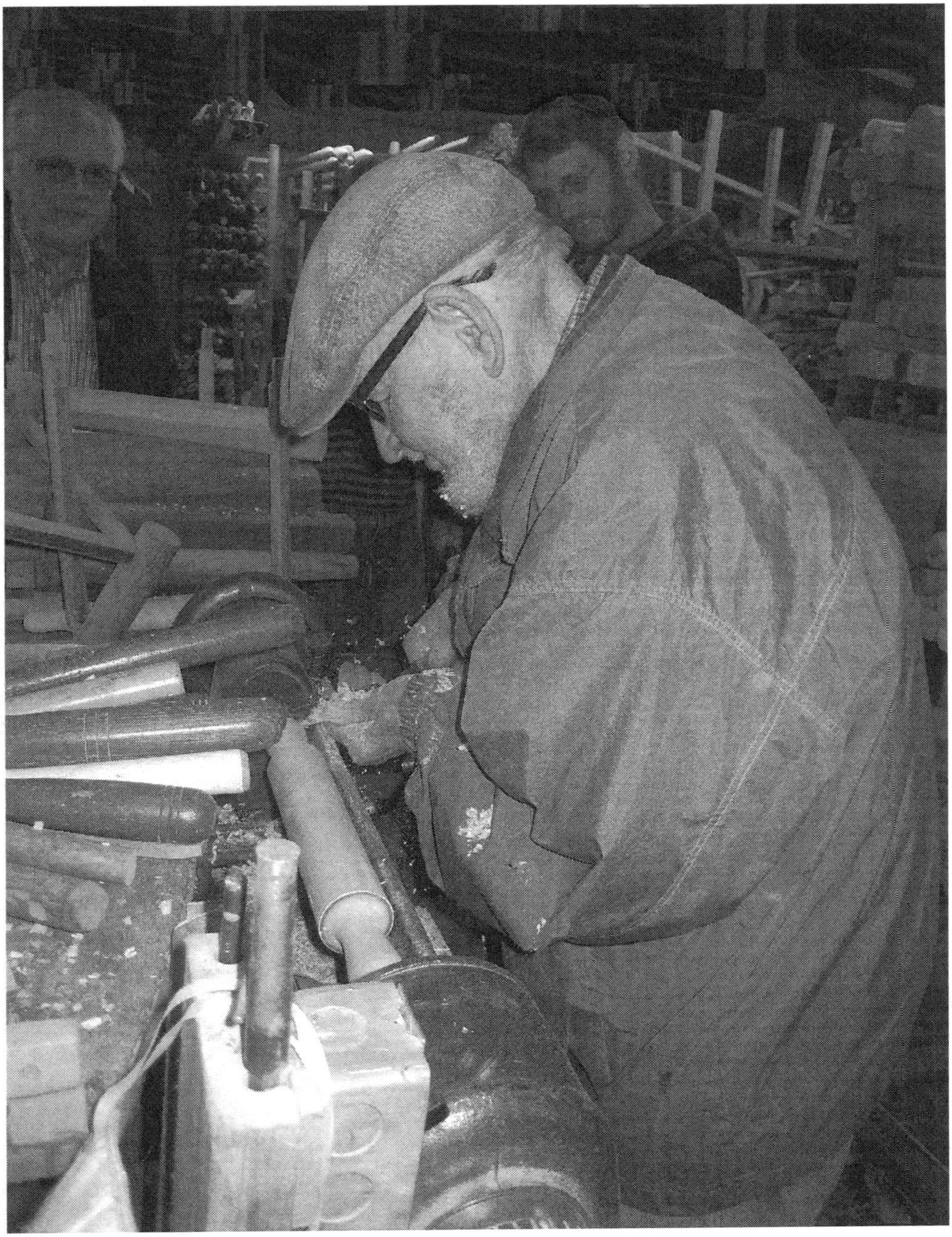

Yet, the stories these tools hold are more than stories of Max and his family, more than stories of making chairs. They hold stories of people who possessed and used the skills they needed to get by, who made the tools they didn't have, and who mended worn tools. Max explains about "up-setting" an ax, the process of adding metal to the worn edge. That repair would be done by someone with skills as a blacksmith, and a barter might be arranged to obtain the needed work. The stories of woodworking go well beyond chairs—to wagons and tool handles, to various improvised responses to need, to roads and bridges, to caskets and more. They are stories of people who came together in times of need, who reached out to each other with supportive hands. These stories remain close to Max's heart, and he gladly shares them.

Max's workshop is a museum of adaptation. In the midst of a generation accustomed to consumption and replacement, Max reminds us of permanence and the value of preservation and conservation. He shows a digging tool that his father made from an old car spring around 1938. Max, too, has cleverly used and reused what was on hand, giving old items new purpose. He reshapes worn files of tungsten steel into chisels. Pieces of wood become a compass to mark the curve of a rocker. This ingenuity that Max uses in making chairs and maintaining his workshop was a part of the lifestyle of his ancestors who worked with wood, made chairs, and even existed because they were able to adapt and to use resources at hand.

Wood and Family

Just as Max came to woodworking through his ancestors, his family has continued to have a hand in chair making. He taught his wife, Pat, to weave fiber rush chair seats along with Max's sister Margaret. Both have greeted visitors at the shop as Max was in the workshop or sharing his chair-making knowledge elsewhere. Max's son Carey also enjoys meeting visitors at the shop. Pat is a steady companion and supporter as she and Max travel to demonstrate the chair-making process.

Max's sister Margaret weaves a chair bottom.
Courtesy of the Max Woody Collection, photographer unknown

Max's wife, Pat, lends a hand at the sanding belt.
Courtesy of the Max Woody Collection, photographer unknown

Max's pride shows through as he speaks of his sons. He hopes that the next Woody generation will continue the legacy of wood that he has honored and carried on. While Carey and Myron both earn higher wages and benefits from furniture industry jobs, they know the importance of their father's chosen path. Through many years, they worked alongside him. Myron has been described by a friend of his dad as "a wizard at making chairs," quick, capable, and insightful. Max recognizes those skills in his son. Myron's work has often taken him overseas, but he hopes to return to Marion someday and use his own capable hands in carrying on the long legacy of wood and chair making. Nothing would please Max Woody more.

Max and his son Myron confer over a chair post.
Courtesy of the Max Woody Collection, photographer unknown

The pole-driven lathe that belonged to Max's great-grandfather, Arthur Woody

Reaching Out

Curious crowds gather around Max as the lathe turns amidst a cloud of woodchips. His able hands shape a chair post, a spindle, or a rolling pin. He often has demonstrated woodturning on his great-grandfather's lathe, first water driven, but now adapted as a spring-pole-driven lathe. He welcomes all who come by, but the young people especially capture his heart.

Even beyond family, Max intends to leave a heritage that remains relevant and vibrant. He is a generous spirit who thrives as he shares his knowledge and skills in numerous settings. Often he has hauled chairs, tools, and pieces of chairs to illustrate the process of chair making and to spark conversation on woodworking, heritage, and whatever serendipity offers.

Max has participated in numerous heritage festivals and similar events where he has shared his work and his knowledge of the older ways of chair making. For 15 years, he enthralled circles of fair-goers at the North Carolina State Fair's Village of Yesteryear. He has been a participant for 38 years at Foxfire's Living History Day (Mountain City, Georgia), at Pioneer Day (Old Fort, North Carolina), and at Turtle Island Preserve (Triplett, North Carolina), to mention only a few venues. For many years, he traveled to Rockingham County to participate in a middle school arts and heritage program, and he has explained the chair-making process through workshops taught at Western Carolina University, Wofford College, Berea College, Warren Wilson College, and Appalachian State University. Similarly, Max has welcomed college students who earned credit as interns in his workshop.

Max eagerly shows steps in the chair making process as groups of youth visit his workshop—Boy Scouts, church groups from nearby denominational retreats, and more. For 15 years, he has taken Outward Bound groups through his workshop and shared with them about his life's

Talking with people who stop by his lathe at Pioneer Day in Old Fort
Courtesy of the Max Woody Collection, photographer unknown

work, but he also talks about direction in life. He encourages them to have a purpose and to follow a path that brings happiness above financial gain. Often, these groups stay overnight at a mountain cabin that Max renovated and expanded.

As Max reflects on times past, he speaks of people from his community, from Raleigh, from Alaska.... Some have held prestigious roles. Some have struggled with life's challenges. Max has offered a hand of kindness and support to others again and again. "A lot of people have helped me along the way," Max says, and gives them credit—people like the teacher Margaret Miller, who helped him earn the last two credits he needed to graduate, and Richard Roberts, the vocational agriculture and shop teacher who filled some gaps after Max's father died. Both remained friends into Max's adult years. Max holds close the memories of his own youthful years, of the kindness and support that helped him move forward on a meaningful path with wood and chairs. Now he extends the same kindness to another generation. As he points out, "You just never know when you are going to touch someone's life for the good. If you can change one person's life, the effort is worthwhile."

Talking about chairs with Max opens a wave of stories about the people he has come to know through wood. He shares stories about people who have enriched his life, but the stories reveal that compassion in Max by which he, too, enriches other's lives. He will talk about letters from youth in the Bronx who have come to the Outward Bound program in the North Carolina mountains. He might even share the file of letters from little girls and newlyweds for whom he has made rolling pins. "Sometimes they even send me a little box of cookies," Max says with a smile.

Max has reached out from his heritage in more ways than chair making. For 30 years, he has helped to bring musicians together weekly to play and enjoy the old music. Max pulls out his fiddle and bow to play along. Old Fort Mountain Music began as a gathering of three musicians among the chairs displayed for sale at Max's workshop. Over time, however, the numbers grew. Now as many as 100 people meet across the road from his workshop on Friday evenings to make music or simply to sit back and enjoy it.

After 64 years as a chair maker, Max still charms observers of all ages with his turning lathe. Hand in hand with his lathe and chairs are his music and stories of the legacy and lifestyle that nurtured his love of wood and chair making. Still, he captures opportunities to talk about direction in life, purpose, and happiness. Max is a giver.

A Heritage of Wood

Claude and Fannie Woody
Courtesy of the Max Woody Collection, photographer unknown

Claude Maxwell Woody, Max's father, made chairs and other wood items but took ten years off from woodworking for a construction job with the Clinchfield Railroad. During this time, he was injured seriously on the job. The family had lived near Forest City in Rutherford County, but the crippling injury and the Depression left Claude jobless and strapped for money. The family lost their home, car, and savings. They moved to McDowell County with just a mule and wagon. Settling 10 miles from Marion in an old, long unoccupied farm house, Claude Woody returned to woodworking despite his physical limitations. Although he could no longer stand to operate a machine, he was able to stand at his workbench, where he worked entirely by hand.

When Max was about 5 years old, his dad made a hickory chair for Max's younger sister, Anna Lee. Working by hand, he used a hand ax to cut the wood pieces, and a knife to even the edges. Finally, he smoothed the surface with broken glass. Pegs hold the chair pieces together. The original seat was made from Max's mother's biscuit board. Later, a cane seat, woven by his mother, replaced the biscuit board.

Despite his crippling injury, distortion from arthritis, and constant pain, Claude Woody's determination and perseverance provided a strong role model for his son. Max remembers his dad tenderly. "I was very close to my dad."

Claude Woody made this hickory chair for his youngest child, Anna Lee. Max and Anna Lee's mother wove the cane seat. *Courtesy of Phil Stroud, photographer and son of Anna Lee Woody Stroud*

Fannie Arrington Woody, Max's mother, wove chair seats and taught workshops on cane weaving for chair seats. Following her husband's disabling injury and continuing after his early death, she worked for 18 years in the Clinchfield Mill to provide for her family of four children. With no transportation for the 10 miles to the mill, she lived with her brother's family in the mill village during the week. When Max and his sisters were able to work and meet family expenses, they brought their mother home for good.

At a Foxfire festival some years later, Max met a man who was doing cane weaving for a chair bottom. "I was surprised to see cane weaving because not many people know how to do it," Max explained, "so I asked him, 'Where did you learn to weave like that?'" He had learned from his grandfather. Later, Max met the grandfather and posed the same question. The man had learned cane weaving from Max's mother in a workshop at Montreat, North Carolina.

Courtesy of the Max Woody Collection, photographer unknown

Max shows the laundry bench that his father made for his mother. When Max's dad faced declining health, the bench became his mother's prayer bench. *Courtesy of the Max Woody Collection, photographer unknown*

Joseph Martin Woody (1875-1964), Max's grandfather, moved from Rutherford County to Marion after the Great Depression cost him his job. He moved in with his son Claude's family and established his chair-making business there. Max Woody learned to make chairs from his granddad.

In his earlier years, Martin Woody made wagons. Later he made chairs, beds, tables, caskets—whatever need called for. If a neighbor needed to replace a broken swingletree (sometimes altered to singletree) so he could continue plowing, Martin put aside his task at hand to make the needed part.

After Max's father died, his grandfather was a strong influence and a primary mentor in woodworking. Stern, not quick to offer praise, this hard-working man provided the example Max needed as he moved toward making chairs himself. When Max announced his intent to make chairs, Martin had been surprised but quickly saw Max's determination and potential in chair-making. Soon after Max began working alongside his granddad in 1950, Martin welcomed Max as a partner in the chair-making business. Max keeps a number of his grandfather's chairs at his own shop.

Max learned how to make chairs from his grandfather. J. M. Woody's Chair Shop stands east of Max's workshop on US 70 West near Marion. J. M. Woody made the deacon's bench. *Courtesy of the Max Woody Collection, photographer unknown*

Martin Woody
Courtesy of the Max Woody Collection, photographer unknown

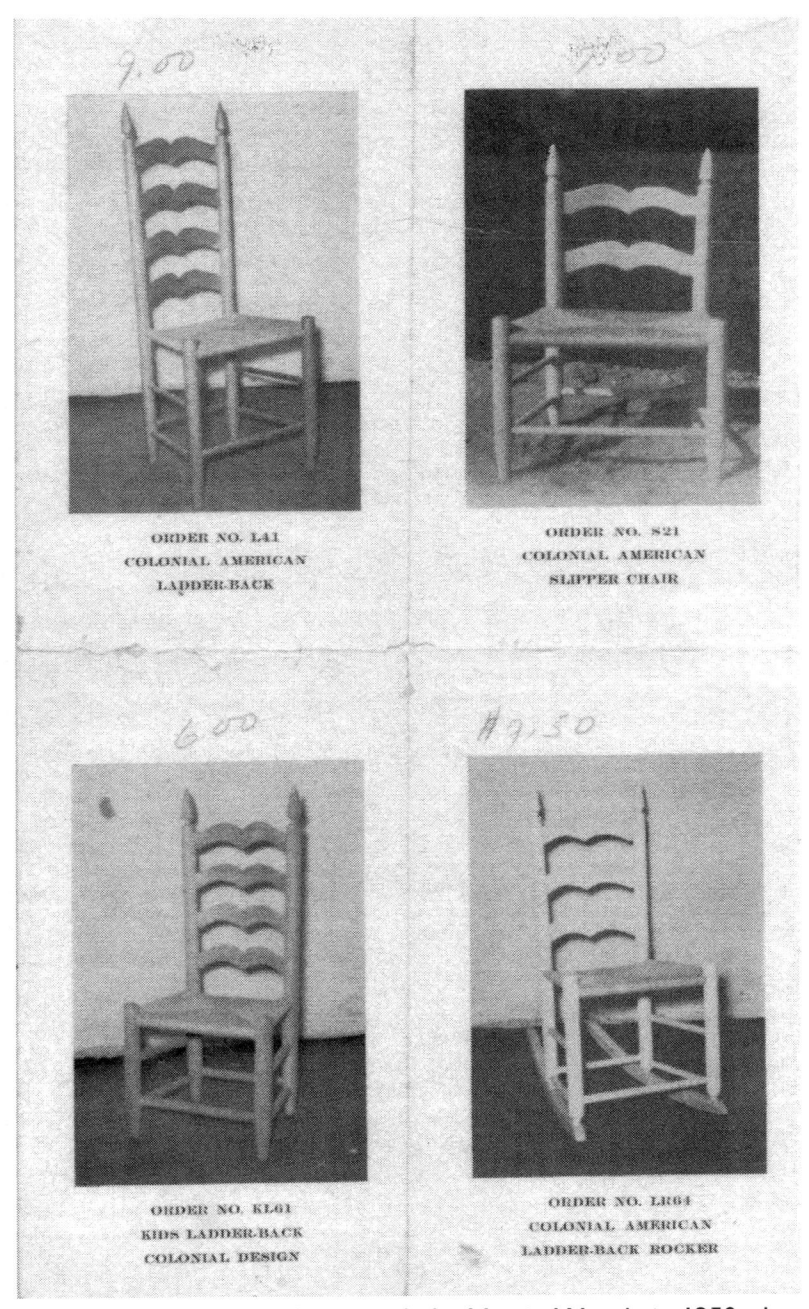

ORDER NO. L41
COLONIAL AMERICAN
LADDER-BACK

ORDER NO. S21
COLONIAL AMERICAN
SLIPPER CHAIR

ORDER NO. KL61
KIDS LADDER-BACK
COLONIAL DESIGN

ORDER NO. LR64
COLONIAL AMERICAN
LADDER-BACK ROCKER

The brochure shows chairs made by Martin Woody in 1950, the year Max began working with him. Notice the handwritten prices.
Courtesy of the Max Woody Collection, photographer unknown

Besides making chairs, Martin Woody spent 20 years working in railroad construction. He supervised a crew that built this wood-framed trestle of locust wood along the CC&O Railroad. The pole frame would be covered with soil, a task accomplished by backing soil-filled ox or mule carts over the trestle and dumping the soil. Cross-ties and tracks were laid across the top. In a parallel, Max also built temporary bridges and culverts with wood and soil for military roads during the Korean War.

This wood trestle, to be filled in as a culvert, was built under Martin Woody's supervision. *Courtesy of the Max Woody Collection, photographer unknown*

Bob Arrington, Max's maternal grandfather, ("Paw"), made chairs, beds and tables. He also made wood caskets, finished with linseed oil, but these were never sold. Often people gathered to help make a casket when a community member died. Women lined the caskets with black or white muslin.

After his mill in Haywood County was washed out during a flood in 1916, Bob Arrington moved his family to McDowell County near Marion. He worked at the Clinchfield Mill for a year and saved money to buy a kerosene engine that would power his mill. He then returned to Haywood County.

Paw provided steady support for Max in the absence of his father. A deeply religious man and a peacemaker, he offered Max wisdom and encouragement. "There are a lot of handy things he said to me," Max recalls.

Courtesy of the Max Woody Collection, photographer unknown

Courtesy of the Max Woody Collection, photographer unknown

Arthur Anderson Woody (1855-1952), Max's great-grandfather, was known to many in his community as "Uncle Arthur." He operated a grist mill and woodworking shop in Mitchell County near Spruce Pine. Arthur's sons Walter and Charles worked with him.

The water wheel powered Arthur's lathe. Max still has the lathe, now converted to a spring-pole lathe. A pole-driven lathe was commonly used when another source of power was not available.

Arthur used a brindled ox named Mike to pull wood down the hillside for his woodworking needs. The ox also pulled a cart to deliver chairs that Arthur made.

Arthur Woody's mill and woodworking shop on Rock House Creek near Spruce Pine. *Courtesy of the Max Woody Collection, photographer unknown*

Arthur Woody learned to make chairs from his father, Wyatt Woody, and from his grandfather, Henry Woody. Although family records stop here, chances are good that these generations, in turn, drew their knowledge of wood and woodworking from their ancestors.

Arthur Woody's son delivers chairs by oxcart to Little Switzerland. *Courtesy of the Max Woody Collection, photographer unknown*

The Legacy
of Max Woody

Sixth Generation Chair Maker
Courtesy of Jon Perry, photographer

Max Woody is determined to pass along his knowledge and skills in woodworking. Unlike a guarded family recipe, the process of making chairs is no secret. Just ask Max. He'll be delighted to tell all about it. For Max, his heritage in wood is something worthy of sharing, worthy of continuing; and in so doing, he makes friend after friend who benefits from Max's wisdom in keeping the older ways. He emphasizes, "Our customers aren't only customers; they are our friends." When Max makes a friend, that friendship is for life.

Max's sons, Myron and Carey, grew up within this legacy of wood. Long before they were old enough to operate a saw, a lathe, or the mortise machine, Max brought them into his workshop. They, too, learned the process and the skills to make chairs as Max has done. They worked alongside Max and became a new link in a long chain of Woody chair makers. Max acknowledges that Myron and Carey missed after-school activities that their friends enjoyed. "They did all they could do," Max says. "I give my boys a lot of credit. They have been many a blessing to me." The heritage that Max knew and the legacy he passed on to Myron and Carey is as familiar to them as their own hands, hands that have mastered the skills that served their ancestors well. Max knows that the legacy in wood is alive in his sons.

What Max has passed on to his sons, and to all who will listen, is not just about a way of making chairs, but also about a way of life, based on community and individuals who share and care for each other. The ways of his parents, grandparents, and great-grandparents provided the model. In those generations, paradoxically, the interaction of persons in the community was essential despite the strong need for families to be self-sufficient.

The spirit of sharing, of caring, of family helping family and neighbor helping neighbor, has long been a part of the legacy that Max inherited and continued. Both through the wood he shapes and the kindness he extends, Max is building a legacy that will continue long past his own days.

Such is the legacy of Max Woody: traditional chairs that last a lifetime or longer, made individually by hand, using time-honored methods; and the perpetuation of knowledge, skills, heritage, community, and friendships. When Max Woody took the leap and bought his first tools in June of 1950, he made an unwavering lifetime commitment, and he has not looked back.

*I don't know what I could have done
that would have given me as much
pleasure as what I have done.*

*I am one of the most blessed people
in the world.*

Seventh Generation Chair Makers Myron at the lathe; Carey finishing a chair. *Courtesy of the Max Woody Collection, photographer unknown*

Max, Zackary, Myron, and Carey
Courtesy of the Max Woody Collection

*Perhaps the tradition
will continue.*

*Zackary, son of Myron
and Ivey Woody, says,
"I'm going to be a chair maker."*

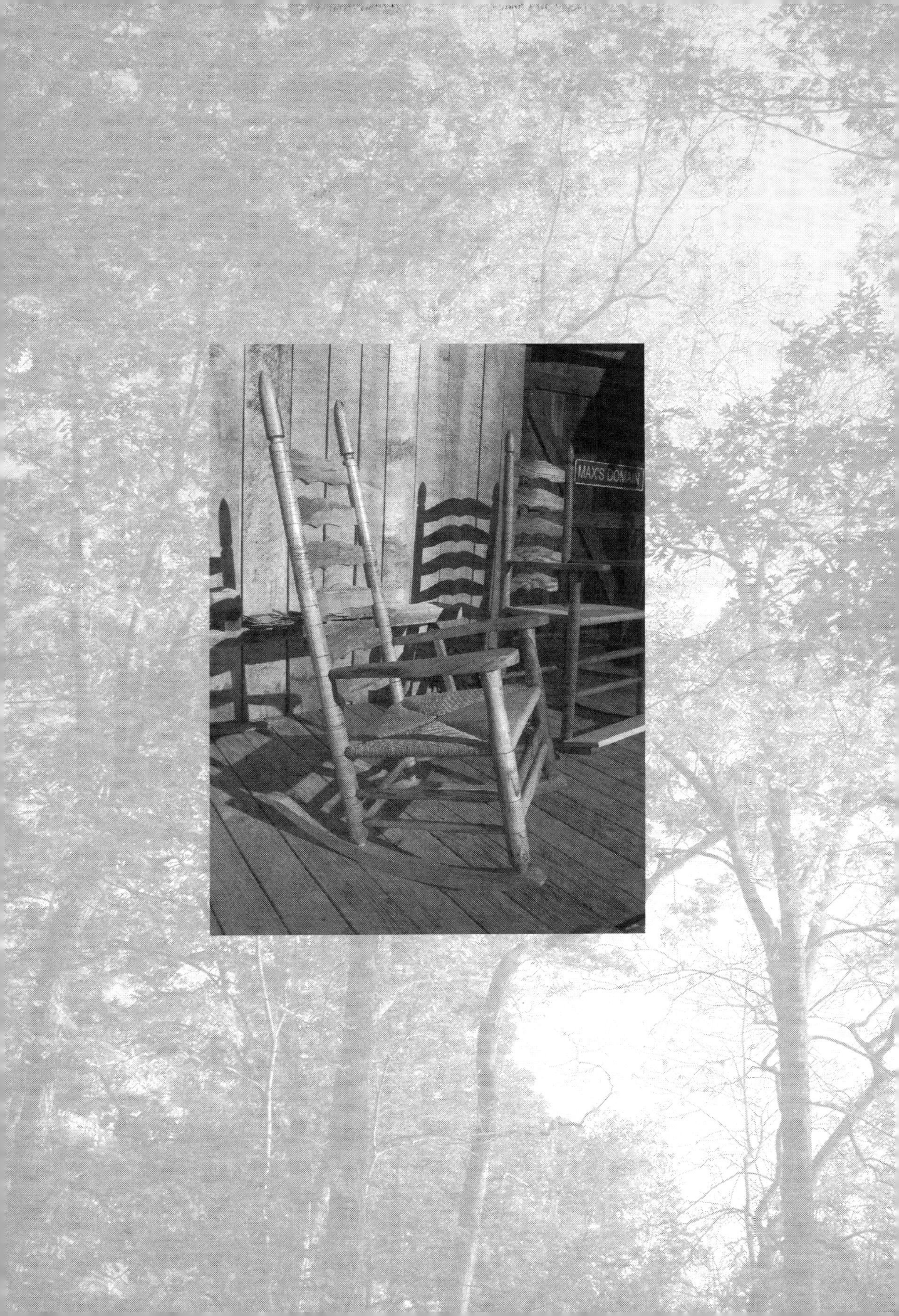
MAX'S DOMAIN

Further Reading About Max Woody

Reynolds, George P. and His Students, eds. "Max and Myron Woody." *Foxfire 10.* New York: Doubleday, 1993. 377-393.

Isbell, Robert. "Chair Maker: Max Woody," *The Keepers.* Winston-Salem, North Carolina: John F. Blair Publisher, 1999. 21-30.

Max reads a list of sales, each handwritten in his record books. The list calls up fond memories and stories of people who bought his chairs.

Visit Max Woody's Chair Shop

The main workshop with sales room:
Max Woody's Chair Shop
3355 US 70 West
Marion, NC 28752
Phone: (828) 724-4158

The showroom and small workshop:
Max Woody Chair Shop
4024 US 221 North
Marion, NC 28752
Phone: (828) 606-7817

About the Author

Julia Taylor Ebel keeps stories of North Carolina people through historical fiction, biography, picture books, folklore, and poetry. Her eight earlier books include *Orville Hicks: Mountain Stories, Mountain Roots; Addie Clawson, Appalachian Mail Carrier;* and *Dresses, Dreams and Beadwood Leaves.* She lives in Jamestown, North Carolina, with her husband and son; but the mountains and mountain people have long captured her heart.

Max Woody is one of those people. His genuine nature, the quality and authenticity of his work, and his unwavering commitment to his legacy create a story that begs to be told.

Courtesy of Jon Perry, photographer

Visit the author's website to learn more about her work in keeping stories.
www.JuliaEbel.com

Made in the USA
Charleston, SC
13 June 2015